Berklee Practice Method

ALTO SAX

AND BARITONE SAX

Get Your Band Together

JIM ODGREN
BILL PIERCE
and the
Berklee Faculty

Berklee Press

Director: Dave Kusek
Managing Editor: Debbie Cavalier
Marketing Manager: Ann Thompson
Sr. Writer/Editor: Jonathan Feist
Writer/Editor: Susan Gedutis
Product Manager: Ilene Altman

ISBN 0-634-00795-5

1140 Boylston Street
Boston, MA 02215-3693 USA
(617) 747-2146

Visit Berklee Press Online at
www.berkleepress.com

DISTRIBUTED BY

HAL•LEONARD®
CORPORATION
7777 W. BLUEMOUND RD. P.O. BOX 13819
MILWAUKEE, WISCONSIN 53213

Visit Hal Leonard Online at
www.halleonard.com

Berklee Practice Method

DESIGN TEAM

Matt Marvuglio	Curriculum Editor
	Dean of the Professional Performance Division
Jonathan Feist	Series Editor
	Senior Writer/Editor, Berklee Press
Rich Appleman	Chair of the Bass Department
Larry Baione	Chair of the Guitar Department
Jeff Galindo	Assistant Professor of Brass
Matt Glaser	Chair of the String Department
Russell Hoffmann	Assistant Professor of Piano
Charles Lewis	Associate Professor of Brass
Jim Odgren	Academic Advising Coordinator
Tiger Okoshi	Associate Professor of Brass
Bill Pierce	Chair of the Woodwind Department
Tom Plsek	Chair of the Brass Department
Mimi Rabson	Assistant Professor of Strings
John Repucci	Assistant Chair of the Bass Department
Ed Saindon	Assistant Professor of Percussion
Ron Savage	Chair of the Ensemble Department
Casey Scheuerell	Associate Professor of Percussion
Paul Schmeling	Chair of the Piano Department
Jan Shapiro	Chair of the Voice Department

The Band

Rich Appleman, Bass
Larry Baione, Guitar
Jim Odgren, Alto Sax
Bill Pierce, Tenor and Soprano Sax
Casey Scheuerell, Drums
Paul Schmeling, Keyboard

Music composed by Matt Marvuglio.
Recording produced and engineered by Rob Jaczko, Chair of the Music Production and Engineering Department.

Contents

CD Tracks

Basics

Chapter I. Playing Rock ("Sweet")

Chapter II. Playing Blues ("Do It Now")

Chapter III. Playing Blues Swing ("I Just Wanna Be With You")

Chapter IV. Playing Funk ("Leave Me Alone")

Foreword

Berklee College of Music has been training musicians for over fifty years. Our graduates go onto successful careers in the music business, and many have found their way to the very top of the industry, producing hit records, receiving the highest awards, and sharing their music with millions of people.

An important reason why Berklee is so successful is that our curriculum stresses the practical application of musical principles. Our students spend a lot of time playing together in bands. When you play with other musicians, you learn things that are impossible to learn in any other way. Teachers are invaluable, practicing by yourself is critical, but performing in a band is the most valuable experience of all. That's what is so special about this series: it gives you the theory you need, but also prepares you to play in a band.

The goal of the *Berklee Practice Method* is to present some of Berklee's teaching strategies in book and audio form. The chairs of each of our instrumental departments—guitar, bass, keyboard, percussion, woodwind, brass, string, and voice—have gotten together and discussed the best ways to teach you how to play in a band. They teamed with some of our best faculty and produced a set of books with play-along audio tracks that uniquely prepares its readers to play with other musicians.

Students who want to study at Berklee come from a variety of backgrounds. Some have great technique, but have never improvised. Some have incredible ears, but need more work on their reading skills. Some have a very creative, intuitive sense of music, but their technical skills aren't strong enough, yet, to articulate their ideas.

The *Berklee Practice Method* teaches many of these different aspects of musicianship. It is the material that our faculty wishes all Berklee freshmen could master before arriving on our doorstep.

When you work through this book, don't just read it. You've got to play through every example, along with the recording. Better yet, play them with your own band.

Playing music with other people is how you will learn the most. This series will help you master the skills you need to become a creative, expressive, and supportive musician that anyone would want to have in their band.

Gary Burton
Executive Vice President,
Berklee College of Music

Preface

Thank you for choosing the *Berklee Practice Method* for saxophone. This book/CD package, developed by the faculty of Berklee College of Music, is part of the *Berklee Practice Method* series—the instrumental method that teaches how to play in a band.

The recording included with this method provides an instant band you can play along with, featuring great players from Berklee's performance faculty. Each tune has exercises and practice tracks that will help prepare you to play it. Rock, blues, and funk are just some of the styles you will perform.

The lessons in this book will guide you through technique that is specific to playing the saxophone in a contemporary ensemble. When you play in a band, your primary concern is with melody and improvisation— how to develop your mastery of phrasing, articulations, breathing, chords, scales, and improvisation techniques. It is intended for saxophone players who can read music and who know the fingerings for most of the notes on the saxophone. These are reviewed in the "Basics" chapter. Ideally, this method should be learned under the guidance of a private teacher, but saxophone players learning on their own will also find it invaluable.

Most important, you will learn the skills you need to play saxophone in a band. Play along with the recording, and play with your friends. This series coordinates methods for many different instruments, and all are based on the same tunes, in the same keys. If you know a drummer, bass player, a guitarist, etc., have them pick up the *Berklee Practice Method* for their own instruments, and then you can jam together.

Work hard, make music, have fun!

Jim Odgren   Bill Pierce
Academic Advising Coordinator   Chair of the Woodwind Department
Berklee College of Music   Berklee College of Music

Basics

Before you start chapter 1, you should understand the following topics.

THE SAXOPHONE FAMILY

There are four types of saxophones that are commonly used: soprano, alto, tenor, and baritone. This book can be used for the E-flat saxophones—the alto and the baritone. The B-flat *Berklee Practice Method* volume is available for the soprano and tenor. The fingering for all saxophones is the same, though the instruments are in different keys. If you read a tenor part on an alto saxophone, the notes will sound on the wrong pitches. For this reason, the music for E-flat instruments is different than the music for B-flat instruments.

B♭ Soprano   E♭ Alto   B♭ Tenor   E♭ Baritone

PARTS OF A SAXOPHONE

There are three parts to a saxophone: the body, the neck, and the mouthpiece. The neck joins the body to the mouthpiece.

Mouthpiece ⟶

Neck

Body

The reed faces downwards, with the flat side against the mouthpiece, and the tip of the reed exactly even with the tip of the mouthpiece. A metal *ligature* holds the reed in place. The mouthpiece should be set far enough into the neck's cork that the saxophone plays in tune.

HOLDING THE SAXOPHONE

The *strap* or *harness* bears the saxophone's weight. Your right thumb rests under the *hook* on the back of the horn towards the bottom. Your left thumb rests on the *thumb rest* on the back of the horn towards the top. Your hands should be relaxed, with only slight forward pressure (never upward pressure) from your thumbs. Your strap and your thumbs should hold the saxophone stable before you place the mouthpiece in your mouth.

Stand up straight. Gravity should pull the saxophone slightly forward. Your playing stance should be stable, comfortable, and allow for freedom of breathing and a balanced hand position. Hold the alto straight out in front of you and the baritone off to your right side.

Holding an Alto

Holding a Baritone

EMBOUCHURE

The position of your mouth is called the *embouchure*. Your top teeth rest lightly on the top of the mouthpiece. Your bottom lip covers your bottom teeth slightly and presses against the reed. The tip of your tongue is tucked behind your bottom teeth. To articulate a note, the top of your tongue (about a quarter-inch past the tip) touches between the reed and the mouthpiece, blocking the space.

TUNING

Before you play, tune your saxophone to the tuning note on the recording. This will ensure that you are in tune when you play along with the recording on the exercises and tunes. Listen to the note on the recording and then play a G (concert B-flat). If you are higher than the recording, pull your mouthpiece out from the neck slightly. If you are lower, then push it in slightly. Find the right position for the mouthpiece so that you can play in tune. If you find that the mouthpiece has to be too far out on the neck in order for you to play in tune, you may be using too much embouchure pressure.

HAND POSITION

Your left fingers cover the top keys and your right fingers cover the bottom keys, as shown.

FINGERINGS

Here are the fingerings for all the notes used in this method. Other fingerings are possible, and if you find them more comfortable, you should feel free to use them instead.

MICROPHONES

If you use a microphone, it should be pointed towards the *bell* (large opening at the end) and placed about six inches away from it. To protect your equipment and your ear drums, follow these steps when you plug your mic into an amp or mixing board.

1. Turn off the amp, and set the volume down to 0.
2. Plug your XLR cable into your mic and then into the amp.
3. Turn on the amp.
4. Play at a medium volume. Slowly, turn up the amp volume until it is loud enough.

NOTATION

Notes are written on a staff.

Saxophone music is written on the "treble clef" staff. Here are the notes for the lines and spaces in treble clef.

Ledger Lines

The staff can be extended with ledger lines.

ACCIDENTALS

Accidentals are symbols appearing before notes, showing that a pitch is raised or lowered for the duration of the measure, unless otherwise indicated.

    ♭   Flat   Next note down (half step down)

    ♯   Sharp   Next note up (half step up)

    ♮   Natural   Cancels a flat or sharp

KEY SIGNATURES

Key signatures indicate a tune's key and show which notes always get sharps or flats. Accidentals on the lines and spaces in the key signature affect those notes throughout the tune unless there is a natural sign. Here are some key signatures used in this book.

C Major   D Major   A Major   E Major
A Minor   B Minor   F♯ Minor   C♯ Minor

RHYTHMS

Below are the basic rhythms. When there are no actual pitches, as in a rhythm-only exercise, rhythms may be shown on the *percussion clef*. (The beats are numbered below the staff.)

Connect notes using a tie. The first note is held for a total of six beats.

Extend a note's rhythmic value by using a dot. A dot increases the value by one half.

Triplets squeeze three even attacks into the space of two. In this example, the quarter-note beat is divided first into two eighth notes, and then into three eighth-note triplets.

RHYTHMIC NOTATION

Music that just shows rhythms may be written in rhythmic notation. This is common in rhythm exercises, where the emphasis is on rhythm, not on which notes you should play. The stems are the same, but the note-heads are different.

| Whole note | Half notes | Quarter notes | Eighth notes | Sixteenth notes |

MEASURES

Groups of beats are divided into measures. Measure lengths are shown with *time signatures*. This measure is in $\frac{4}{4}$ time—there are four beats in the measure, and the quarter note gets the beat.

In $\frac{12}{8}$ time, there are twelve beats per measure and the eighth note gets the beat. (Often, $\frac{12}{8}$ is felt as four beats, with three lesser beats inside each.)

Now, let's play!

"Sweet" is a *rock* tune. Rock started in the 1960s and has roots in blues, swing, r&b, and rock 'n' roll. There are many different styles of rock. To hear more rock, listen to artists such as Rage Against the Machine, Melissa Etheridge, Korn, Paula Cole, Bjork, Tori Amos, Primus, Jimi Hendrix, and Led Zeppelin.

LESSON 1
TECHNIQUE/THEORY

Listen to "Sweet" on the recording. This tune has two parts.

In the first part of the melody, the saxophone plays these notes. Use your ear to find the rhythms.

In the second part, the saxophone plays these notes.

Play along with the recording, and try to match the melody. Notice that there is a short introduction before the first part begins.

MELODY

Melodies such as "Sweet" are created out of different *licks*—short, melodic figures or *phrases*. A musical phrase is similar to a phrase in spoken or written language. It is a continuous musical idea that is unbroken and uninterrupted by long rests or periods of silence. Phrases can be short licks, or they can be extended melodies.

In "Sweet," the saxophone and lead guitar play the melody, and the other instruments play other kinds of parts. The parts all sound good together because the melody, the *chords* (three or more notes sounded together), and the *groove* (rhythmic time-feel) all work together.

ARTICULATION

Articulation is the way a note is played—short, long, accented, and so on. Choosing good articulations for your notes and phrases will make your melodies come alive.

On a saxophone, different articulations are played by changing your breathing and your tonguing. Changing the way you *attack* (start) and *release* (stop) the sound changes the note's articulation.

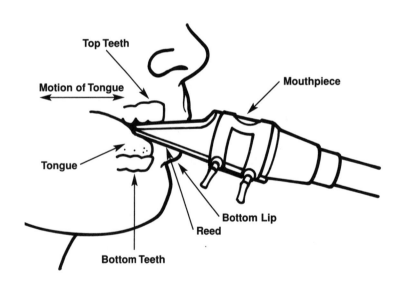

Legato

Notes in the first part of "Sweet" flow together smoothly. This is *legato* style articulation, often notated with a *slur* marking (⌒). Each note is held for its *full rhythmic value* so that it leads right up to the next note. Only breathe between phrases.

When you attack a legato note, your tongue should move lightly, as if you were saying "tah," touching the tip of the reed for the T sound, as if it was the back of your top teeth. Each articulation should happen a split second before the note sounds. There should be almost no space between notes.

Practice legato long tones with the recording. Only breathe every two measures, where you see a breath mark ('). Count in your head while you play, and make sure you hold each note for its full value.

Practice the first part of "Sweet" using legato articulation, using the same track. The notes within each phrase should sound connected.

Staccato

Notes in the second part to "Sweet" are much shorter and more separated. The opposite of legato (long) is *staccato* (short). Staccato notes are indicated with a dot (.). To play staccato, attack the note with the same T tongue motion, but then end it quickly, as in the word "tut." The attack is actually a release of the air pressure. The tongue releases the air, with the consonant T starting and stopping the sound.

Staccato notes are not held for their full rhythmic value, and there should be space between notes. Staccato quarter notes are written like this:

The notes sound much shorter than quarter notes—more like sixteenths. Here is the same line written as sixteenth notes. As you can see, the dots are much easier to read than the sixteenth-note flags with dotted eighth-note rests.

Practice staccato articulations with the recording, one note per beat. Only breathe every two measures, where you see a breath mark. Though the notes are short, you should still think about phrasing, and breathe between phrases rather than between notes. Keep your air moving.

Now practice staccato eighth notes with the recording. Keep using that "tut" syllable.

The licks in the second part of "Sweet" each have three notes that are played staccato on the recording. The other notes shouldn't be as short. Practice these licks a few times to get the staccato feel, and then practice it with the recording.

> ### PRACTICE TIP
>
> Remember to keep the tip of your tongue tucked behind your bottom teeth. If you play short notes and long notes, it will be much easier to play accurate rhythms and stay in the groove.

LEAD SHEETS

Articulations may be marked in formal, published music. When you play in a band, more often, you will use informal music that only shows chord symbols and melody, usually with no articulations, no phrasing, and no other expressive markings. This is called a *lead sheet*. Finding the right articulations will be up to you.

This is what the first part to "Sweet" looks like on a lead sheet.

The whole band may read the same lead sheet. Each player will use it differently to create a part for their instrument. As a saxophone player, one way you will use the lead sheet is to read and play the song's melody.

The piano, guitar, and bass all play parts using notes from the chords. By tuning in to the chords, you'll find it easier to keep your place in the music. When it's your turn to *solo* (improvise), the chord symbols will be useful to you as well, as we will see in later chapters.

Different bands will create different parts for the same tune. This is one of the coolest things about lead-sheet notation: it leaves room for individual interpretation.

You will see the full lead sheet to "Sweet" in lesson 4.

LESSON 2
LEARNING THE GROOVE

WHAT IS A GROOVE?

A *groove* is a combination of musical patterns in which everyone in the band feels and plays to a common pulse. This creates a sense of unity and momentum. The *rhythm section* (usually drums, bass, guitar, and keyboard) lays down the groove's dynamic and rhythmic feel. A singer, saxophonist, or other soloist also contributes to the groove, and performs the melody based on this feel.

Listen to "Sweet." As is common in hard rock, the groove to "Sweet" has a strong, clear pulse and a loud, forceful sound. The drums play a heavy, repetitive beat. The bass outlines the harmonic structure. The rhythm guitar and keyboard play chords. The sax and lead guitar play the melody. Everyone uses the same rhythms, though often at different times. This makes the whole band sound like one unit; they're all *hooked up* with the groove.

In lesson 1, when you played along with the recording and matched the saxophone part, you hooked up with a groove and became part of the band.

SAX IN A GROOVE

On our recording of "Sweet," the saxophonist has two roles in the groove: melody and improvisation. If there were several horn players (saxophones, trumpets, trombones, and so on), there might be a third kind of role—that of a member of a horn section. In a section, the horns may play chords together, or they may all play the same melody in *unison* (at the same time). In a smaller band, there may be only one sax player. He would be *out front*, and at the center of attention.

As a sax player, you are not a member of the rhythm section, but you are still part of the groove, and must tap into its rhythmic feel. The way that you play the melody should help the other band members feel the beat or pulse you feel.

HOOKING UP TO ROCK

The way to hook up to a groove is by learning its unique pulse and rhythmic feel. Then, your playing will hook up rhythmically with the rest of the band.

Your phrasing and articulation will help you define the rhythms of the melody and hook up to the groove. Move your fingers evenly over the keys. Open and close the keys with gentle but deliberate motions. This will help you to hook up.

> ### PRACTICE TIP
>
> When you learn a groove, start out by clicking out the rhythms only, without blowing into your instrument. To click rhythms while you are holding your saxophone, click all the right-hand keys shut at the same time so they make a "pop" sound. Don't slam them too hard! You might damage the pads. When you release the keys, you will get another click.

Count along with the beat, repeating "1, 2, 3, 4" through every measure. While you count, click the keys along with the snare drum on the *backbeat*—beats 2 and 4, where you see the circles below. A strong backbeat is one of the characteristics of rock grooves.

While you click and count, tap your foot on the quarter-note pulse.

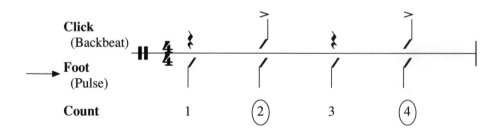

This tune has a sixteenth-note feel, so change your counting to sixteenth notes, matching the cymbals. On each beat, count evenly, "1 e + a, 2 e + a, 3 e + a, 4 e + a" (say "and" for "+"). Try saying this first at a slower tempo, without the recording, until you get the hang of it. When you are ready, play the recording and say the syllables in tempo.

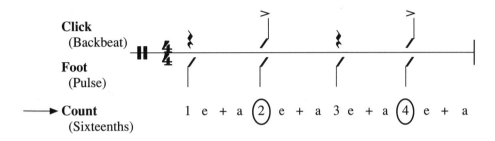

Click your keys in the rhythm of the saxophone's melody during the first part to "Sweet." Tap your foot, and feel the sixteenth-note *subdivisions* (divisions within a beat). When you are ready, click along with the recording. The same phrase is played twice.

Play the actual part along with the recording. Tap your foot and feel the sixteenth notes as you play. Use legato articulations, and hook up with the groove.

LISTEN 3 PLAY

Listen to the second part to "Sweet," find the pulse, and count along. Then, click the saxophone rhythms of the second part (use the keys' release sound as another click so that you can do it faster). When you are ready, click along with the recording. The same rhythmic lick repeats, played a total of eight times.

LISTEN 4 PLAY

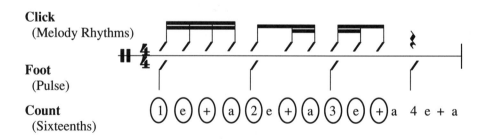

Play the actual part along with the recording. Tap your foot and count in your head as you play. Use staccato articulations, and hook up with the groove.

Finally, play both parts together, following your ear and not looking at the music. Make sure to use different articulations on each part, and hook up with the rhythm section. When the sax solos, sit back and listen. Come in again when the melody returns.

LESSON 3
IMPROVISATION

Improvisation is the invention of a solo. When you improvise, you tell the story of what you think about the tune and what it means to you. Though an improvised solo may seem spontaneous to the audience, the musician probably did a lot of preparation before performing it. There are three things you must know before you start improvising: the song melody, when you should solo, and what notes will sound good in your solo.

FORM AND ARRANGEMENT

When you are preparing to improvise on a tune, start by learning how it is organized. This will let you know when you should start your improvised solo and where the chords change.

LISTEN 2 PLAY

Listen to "Sweet," and follow the saxophone. After an introduction by the rhythm section, the sax plays the melody. Then, there is an improvised sax solo. Finally, the sax plays the melody again, followed by a short ending.

During the improvised solo, you can still feel the written melody. That's because the improvisation follows the same chords as the written melody. This repeating chord pattern is the same throughout the entire tune, and is called the song's *form*—its plan or structure.

A common way to show this organization is with a *chord chart*. Chord charts don't show rhythm or pitch, just measures and chord symbols. The slash marks (/ / / /) mean "play in time."

The chord chart makes it easy to see that the form of "Sweet" is sixteen measures long. It has two primary musical ideas: the first eight measures present the first idea (Idea "A"), with the **C♯– F♯ C♯–** patterns. The second eight measures present the second idea (Idea "B"), with the **F♯– B F♯– B** patterns. This form can be described simply as "AB" or "AB form." These letters help us remember the form, freeing us from having to read while we're performing.

HEAD/CHORUS

One complete repetition of this form is called a *chorus*. A chorus can feature the written melody, in which case it is called the *head*, or it can feature just the chord structure, supporting an improvisation. (The word *chorus* is also used to mean a song section that is alternated with varying verses. In this book, however, the word "chorus" is only used to mean "once through the form.")

ARRANGING "SWEET"

Your band can choose how many choruses you want to play and create your own *arrangement* of "Sweet." The number of choruses depends on how many players will improvise when you perform the tune. On the recorded performance of "Sweet," only one player solos (the sax), playing for two choruses. Often, several members of the band will take turns playing choruses of improvised solos. A solo can be one or two choruses, or even more.

On the recording, the same basic arrangement is used for all the tunes: the head, an improvised sax solo, and then the head again. There are often short introductions and endings as well.

Listen to "Sweet" and follow the arrangement. This is the arrangement for "Sweet" played on the recording:

INTRO	HEAD	SAX SOLO: 2x	HEAD	ENDING
4 MEASURES	‖ 1 CHORUS = 16 MEASURES ‖:	1 CHORUS = 16 MEASURES :‖	1 CHORUS = 16 MEASURES ‖	2 MEASURES ‖

When you play "Sweet" with your band, you can play your own arrangement, adding extra solo choruses, different endings, or other changes.

IDEAS FOR IMPROVISING

When you improvise, some notes will sound better than others. There are many ways to find notes that will sound good. You can use the notes from the tune's melody, you can use notes from the chords, and you can use notes from scales that match the tune. Eventually, this becomes intuitive, and you can just follow your ear.

SCALES: C-SHARP MINOR PENTATONIC

The saxophone player on this recording of "Sweet" built much of his solo using notes from a *pentatonic scale*. Pentatonic scales are among the simplest and most versatile types of scales in all of music. All pentatonic scales have five notes. There are two common types of pentatonic scales: major and minor. For "Sweet," the soloist used the *minor pentatonic scale* built on C-sharp. This scale works well here because the tune is in the key of C-sharp minor. Notice that the C-sharp is repeated, up an octave, to close the scale.

Use this scale to create your improvised licks. You only need a few notes to create a lick, so divide the scale into halves. Use one half for some licks and the other half for other licks. This will add contrast between them.

Group 1   # Group 2

Here are some of the licks that can be created using some notes from these groups.

You may have noticed that all of these licks use the same rhythm. This is the rhythm used above.

Plugging different notes into the same rhythm is another good technique for building solos. It makes the licks sound related, like part of the same thing. You don't need to use the same exact rhythm every time, but some repetition can be very effective.

CALL AND RESPONSE

Listen to each phrase, and then play it back, echoing it exactly. Each lick comes from the C-sharp minor pentatonic scale, using the groupings and the rhythm discussed above. Slashes ("✓") in measures marked "play" mean that you should play in time during those measures. Listen carefully, and hook up with the groove.

Keep practicing that track until you can echo all phrases perfectly. Then do the same thing for the phrases on this next track.

LISTEN 5,6 PLAY

Play the same two tracks again. This time, instead of echoing the phrases exactly, answer them with your own improvised phrases. Use the same rhythms, and only use notes of the C-sharp minor pentatonic scale.

Write out some of your own licks, like the ones you have been playing. Don't worry about perfecting your notation; just sketch out your ideas. This will help you remember them when you are improvising.

LISTEN 7 PLAY

Create a 1-chorus solo using any techniques you have learned. Memorize your solo, and practice it along with the recording.

PLAY IN A BAND TIP

When playing in a band, listen to the other players' parts and try to create a musical conversation. This makes playing much more fun, and more musical too. When you are improvising a solo, listen to what the other instruments are playing. They will suggest many ideas that you can use in your solo, such as rhythms and licks, and you will inspire each other.

LESSON 4
READING

When you play in a band, sometimes, you will get a keyboard part for the tune that shows exactly what you should play. Other times, you will get a lead sheet, giving you more freedom to create your own part. You should be able to play from either one.

SAXOPHONE PART

Below is a written E-flat saxophone part to "Sweet." This part shows articulation markings and rehearsal letters.

HARD ROCK	Style indication. This tune is hard rock, and you should play it in that style: heavy bass, strong beat, sixteenth-note feel, and other elements typical of that hard-edged sound.
♩ = 86	Metronome marking. This tells you how fast you should play this tune. If you have a metronome, set it to 86, and play "Sweet" at that tempo.
INTRO	Introduction. The written part begins with an introduction, which is made up of four measures of the B section.
3 ▬	A bar with a number over it means that you should rest for that number of measures. The introduction begins with just the rhythm section, so you can sit out. But count along, so you are ready to come in on the pickup to letter A.
[A]	Rehearsal letter. These are different than form letters, which you saw in lesson 3. These letters help you when you are practicing with other musicians because everyone's parts have the same letters marked at the same places.
‖: :‖	Repeat signs. Play the music between these signs twice (or more).
[A9]	Rehearsal letter with measure number. These mark different areas within a chorus. Again, this can be helpful during rehearsals.
AFTER SOLOS, REPEAT TO ENDING	When the soloists are finished, play the head one more time, and then proceed to the measures marked "Ending."
ENDING	A final section that is added to the form. End the tune with these measures.

Play "Sweet" along with the recording. Follow the saxophone part exactly as it is written.

Sweet
Eb Saxophone Part
By Matt Marvuglio

LEAD SHEET

Lead sheets present the chords and melody. They give you a little more interpretive freedom than full formal saxophone parts do. Notice that there is no written introduction on this lead sheet. The introduction you hear in the recording is an interpretation of the lead sheet by that band. Your band should create your own unique arrangement.

PLAY IN A BAND TIP

As you rehearse "Sweet," follow the lead sheet. It will help you keep your place in the form.

CHAPTER I
DAILY PRACTICE ROUTINE

ARTICULATION PRACTICE

Legato

Practice these two legato exercises along with the recording to the first part of "Sweet." Breathe only where you see the breath marks. The notes should sound almost connected to each other.

> ### PRACTICE TIP
>
> When you begin a legato note, move your tongue as if you were saying "tah." At the end of each phrase, imagine that you are saying "hut," seemlessly blending the H of "hut" with the H of "tah." This will help you sustain your breath support and define the phrase ending.

LISTEN **3** PLAY

Legato Exercise 1

Legato Exercise 2

Staccato

Practice the C-sharp minor pentatonic scale along with the recording, using staccato articulations. Listen to the drums, and try to play your notes exactly in time.

Staccato Exercise 1

Staccato Exercise 2

SCALE PRACTICE

Here are the notes of the C-sharp minor pentatonic scale through two octaves. When you are comfortable playing all of these notes, you'll be able to use them when you improvise.

In lesson 3, you divided the scale into two groups of three notes. There are other ways to group notes of this scale. For example, you can take groups of four consecutive scale notes, beginning on any scale degree. This next exercise shows you many different ways of grouping notes, and helps you master the C-sharp minor pentatonic scale throughout the saxophone's register. Practice it with both legato and staccato phrasing. Breathe only at the breath marks. This exercise is based on the complete form of "Sweet," so you can practice it along with the extended track, playing it several times. Begin after the introduction.

IMPROVISATION PRACTICE

This exercise will help you practice improvising. You will use groups of notes from the C-sharp minor pentatonic scale and a rhythmic pattern, just like you did in lesson 3. The difference is that now you will be creating improvised licks while the music is playing.

Before you play, you must do two things. First, you must choose your groups of notes. For now, we'll use the same groups from lesson 3.

Group 1   # Group 2

Second, you must choose a rhythmic figure. Again, we'll start with the one from lesson 3.

Here's how it works. You will be improvising with the rhythm section. In odd measures, you will play; in even measures, you will plan. When you plan, decide what you will play, choosing what notes to use in the rhythm above, choosing notes alternately from groups 1 and 2. Before you begin, plan your first measure. It will be organized like this:

When you are comfortable with that, use different groups of notes and different rhythms. For groups of notes, choose some from the pentatonic exercise earlier in this section. For rhythms, you can use any of these, or write your own. Just keep it simple, and be strict in following it.

CHALLENGE

Choose different rhythms or note groups for the A section and for the B section. When you play along with the track, play the melody at the first and last chorus, as it is played in the recording.

MEMORIZE

Memorizing the licks and melodies from these exercises will help you play the tune, especially when you improvise. What you practice helps you when you perform. But performing is the best practice, so get together with some other musicians and learn these tunes with your own band.

Memorize the saxophone part to "Sweet." Also memorize the lead sheet. The "Summary" shows everything you need to play "Sweet" from a lead sheet. Memorizing it will help you memorize the tune.

> ### PRACTICE TIP
>
> Write out your own exercises based on the C-sharp minor pentatonic scale. The more ways you find to make melodies from that scale, the more you make music that's truly your own!

SUMMARY

FORM
16-BAR AB
(1 CHORUS = 16 BARS)
A: 8 M.
B: 8 M.

ARRANGEMENT
INTRO: 4 M.
1 CHORUS MELODY
2 CHORUS SOLO
1 CHORUS MELODY
END: 2 M.

HARMONY
A C#– F# B F#– B

SCALE
C# MINOR PENTATONIC

PLAY "SWEET" WITH YOUR OWN BAND!

"Do It Now" is a *blues* tune. Blues began in the late 1800s, and it has had a profound influence on American music styles, including rock, jazz, and soul. To hear more blues, listen to artists such as B.B. King, the Blues Brothers, Robben Ford, Bonnie Raitt, James Cotton, Albert King, and Paul Butterfield.

LESSON 5
TECHNIQUE/THEORY

Listen to the recording of "Do It Now," and play along. Try to match the saxophones, which are doubled by the guitar. The melody has three lines. Each starts differently, but ends the same.

PRACTICE TIP

In melodies, look for patterns—notes that are the same or similar from one phrase to the next. In "Do It Now," the three lines end exactly the same. Also, the first two are very similar, with the only difference being that the first F-sharp in the first line changes to an F-natural in the second. As you learn songs, notice what remains the same and what's different. You'll learn them faster.

BREATHING

When you play a phrase, you need to have enough air (breath) in your lungs for the whole phrase. It should feel as natural to you as saying a complete sentence in one breath. You don't run out of air when you speak, so you shouldn't run out of air when you play!

Inhale before you begin playing. Develop the habit of breathing *during the count-off*, before you begin.

Here's how it works for a tune like "Do It Now." This tune begins on beat 1 of the first measure. During the measure leading up to where you play, exhale during beats 1 and 2, and then inhale during beats 3 and 4.

PRACTICE TIP

A full breath will help you produce a big, full saxophone sound.

BREATH MARKS

In chapter 1, you saw the breath mark symbol ('). Most music won't include these, so you have to write them in yourself. Try to plan your breathing so that you can play complete phrases without interruption.

Play the first phrase of the melody along with the recording, and only breathe at the marks. Make your breaths even, and don't trim too much time off of the whole notes. Next, try playing through the first mark, and only breathe at the end of the 4-measure phrase.

When a melody has many long notes, plan your breathing so that you can hold all notes for their full duration. Inhale deeply so that you will have enough air for the end of the phrase. If you are running out of air, try to find an additional place to breathe, so that the sound remains strong throughout the phrase.

WRITE IN YOUR OWN BREATH MARKS

Below is the entire melody of "Do It Now." Play through it, and write in your own breath marks. Try to preserve the melody's natural phrases, and be sure you can maintain a strong sound throughout. Practice it along with the recording. Change your markings if you think you can improve them.

LESSON 6
LEARNING THE GROOVE

HOOKING UP TO A BLUES SHUFFLE

LISTEN **8** PLAY

Listen to "Do It Now." This groove has its roots in traditional r&b, gospel, and jazz. The feel is often called a $\frac{12}{8}$ *shuffle* because of the twelve eighth notes in each bar. (The drums play these on the ride cymbal and hi-hat.)

Tap your foot on every beat, and count triplets: "1 trip-let 2 trip-let 3 trip-let 4 trip-let." The basic pulse (tap) is on the quarter note. However, each pulse also has an underlying triplet that divides the beat into three equal parts:

This triplet feel is part of what makes the beat a *shuffle*. While all shuffles don't include triplets on every single beat, the underlying triplet *feel* is always present.

The triplet is a fundamental aspect of all swing and shuffle beats. Understanding and feeling the concept of subdivisions (dividing the pulse into smaller rhythms) will help you play many other kinds of grooves.

"Do It Now" begins with the drums playing two beats of triplets. This establishes the shuffle groove. Listen for the steady triplet beat in the hi-hat, and find the triplet patterns in the other instruments. Listen to the bass part. Which beats have a triplet feel? Is the triplet pattern the same in every measure or does it change?

SWING EIGHTH NOTES

Eighth notes in shuffle grooves are usually played as triplets, even though they are notated as *straight* eighth notes.

Though these rhythms look different, in some musical styles, they are played the same. The notated part to "Do It Now" shows eighth notes notated like this:

Since it is a shuffle tune, they are played more like this:

The part is easier to read without the triplet markings on every beat, and the rhythms are played as triplets even though they are notated as if they were regular eighth notes. Interpreting rhythms in this way is called "swinging the eighth notes." Swing eighth notes are common in many styles of music, including blues, jazz, and swing.

Sometimes, the word "swing," "swing feel," or "shuffle" appears on the lead sheet, telling you how to play eighth notes. If there is no such indication, try it both ways and choose which fits the groove best. The style of the tune may help you choose whether to swing your eighth notes or play them straight.

Listen again to "Do It Now," and play the saxophone part along with the recording. Feel the triplets on every beat, listen to the drums, and hook up with the groove.

LESSON 7
IMPROVISATION

FORM: 12-BAR BLUES

Listen to "Do It Now," and follow the form. The form of this tune is called a *12-bar blues*.

A 12-bar blues has three 4-bar phrases. It is common for the first two phrases in the melody to be similar and the third one to be different. This form is very common in many styles of music, including jazz, rock, and funk.

In "Do It Now," the first phrase has four bars of the I chord (**D7**). The second phrase has two bars of the IV chord (**G7**) followed by two bars of the I chord (**D7**). The third section has one bar of V (**A7**), one bar of IV (**G7**), and then two bars of I (**D7**). This is typically the way that chords move in blues.

Memorize the blues form and chord progression. You will see it again many times throughout your career.

ARRANGEMENT

"Do It Now" begins with the drum playing two beats of triplets. This is called a *pickup*—a short introduction, less than a measure long, that leads to a strong downbeat. The tenor sax joins the alto on the head. Here is the arrangement played on the recording.

PICKUP	HEAD: 2x	SAX SOLO: 2x	HEAD	ENDING
2 Beats Drums	‖: 1 Chorus = 12 Measures :‖	‖: 1 Chorus = 12 Measures :‖	1 Chorus = 12 Measures	4 Measures ‖

PRACTICE TIP

When you listen to any music, figure out the arrangement. How long is the head? Is there an introduction or an ending? How many solo choruses does the band take?

SCALES: D BLUES

In chapter 1, you created bass lines using the C-sharp minor pentatonic scale. Here is the D minor pentatonic scale.

The *D blues scale* has just one more note—the flat fifth degree (A-flat or G-sharp).

Practice the D blues scale over a two-octave range on your saxophone.

CALL AND RESPONSE

In these call-and-response exercises, divide the D blues scale into two groups. The A-flat will be used in both groups. The first chorus draws from group 1, and the second chorus draws from group 2. The notes of each group can be played in any octave.

Group 1   Group 2

Use this rhythm for each lick.

1. Echo each lick, exactly as you hear it.
2. Improvise an answer to each lick. Use the same rhythm for each answer, but choose your own notes.

Use notes from group 1 in this chorus.

Use notes from group 2 in this chorus.

Use notes from groups 1 or 2 in this chorus, choosing the same group as you hear on the recording.

Write out a few of your own ideas. Use the D blues scale.

Create a 2-chorus solo using any techniques you have learned. Memorize your solo, and practice it along with the recording.

LESSON 8
READING

SAXOPHONE PART

This *chart* (written part) uses symbols and instructions that direct you to skip around the pages. When you get the hang of these symbols, you will see that they help reduce the number of written measures and make the chart easier to read quickly, at a glance. Sometimes, these directions are called the chart's *road map*.

BASS PART   Bass Part. Sometimes, you will see other instruments, especially when it is optional for the sax to double them. A baritone saxophone can be a good substitute for a bass, if your band is looking for a different color. Note that this is a transposed part. If a bass player were to read it, he would have to transpose it so that the notes would be right.

2 BEATS DRUMS   Pickup. Short introduction (less than a measure).

𝄋   Sign. Later, there will be a direction (D.S., or "from the sign") telling you to jump to this symbol from another location in the music.

⊕   Coda symbol. "Coda" is another word for "ending." On the last chorus, skip from the first coda symbol to the second coda symbol (at the end of the piece). This symbol may also have the words "To Coda," or other directions (such as "last time only"). Often, you will just see the coda symbol by itself.

D.S. AL ⊕   From the sign (𝄋), and take the coda. Jump back to the sign (first measure, after the pickup), and play from there. When you reach the first coda symbol, skip ahead to the next coda symbol (at the end).

AFTER SOLOS   When all solo choruses are finished, follow this direction.

B̲   Different choruses may be marked with different letters. In this tune, the head is marked "A," and the improvisation choruses are marked "B."

SOLO   Solo chorus. Play this part when other musicians in the band improvise. When you play this tune with your own band, you might repeat this section several times, depending on how many people solo. When you solo, then obviously, you won't play this written part.

Play "Do It Now" along with the recording, and follow the written saxophone part exactly. Even if you have it memorized already, follow the part as you play.

Do It Now

Eb Saxophone Part

By Matt Marvuglio

LEAD SHEET

Now play "Do It Now" with the recording, and work from the lead sheet.

CHAPTER II
DAILY PRACTICE ROUTINE

BLUES SCALE PRACTICE

Saxophone Register: High Notes/Low Notes

Playing in different registers will give you new tone qualities and sounds. A phrase played in the low register has a certain energy and intensity. The same phrase played an octave higher will have a different feel and sound.

Practice this register exercise, and when you are ready, practice it along with the recording. Notice the different characters between the registers.

SAXOPHONE PLAYERS AND CHORDS

Guitar and keyboard players often play *chords*—three or more notes sounded simultaneously. Since the saxophone can only sound one note at a time, it can only play the notes one after another, or as *arpeggios*. If you have three or more saxophones, then the section can play chords together.

"Do It Now" uses three different *dominant seventh* chords in its chord progression. Play them on your saxophone.

Chord tones (the notes of a chord) are important resources for notes when you improvise, similar to scales. Practice playing the chord tones for the chords in "Do It Now," using rhythms that fit the song's feel. Remember to swing your eighth notes. When you are ready, play this exercise along with the recording.

SEVENTH CHORD EXERCISE 2

These exercises will help you develop your skills playing dominant seventh chords. (Baritone sax players may prefer to transpose some notes of the first exercise down an octave.) It is in *descending form*—moving from high to low. Swing your eighth notes. Practice each chorus until you can play it easily, and then practice it with the recording.

The second exercise presents dominant seventh chords in *ascending form*—moving from low to high.

SOLO PRACTICE

Practice the first chorus of the solo to "Do It Now" along with the recording, reading the noteheads below. Use your ear to find the right rhythms.

LISTEN **8** PLAY

LISTEN **12** PLAY

When you can play this solo, play the full tune without looking at the music—first the melody, then the solo (play the above chorus twice), and then the melody again to end it. Follow your ear, and try to match the sax on the recording.

PERFORMANCE TIP

If you make a mistake or get lost, keep your composure, and pretend that everything is going fine. Listen to the other instruments, hear what chords they are playing, and find your way back into the form. You can even practice getting lost and then finding your place. Start the recording at a random point within the track, and then follow your ear.

MEMORIZE

Create your own solo using any techniques you have learned. Memorize your part, and then play through the tune with the recording as if you were performing it live. Keep your place in the form, and don't stop, whatever happens.

SUMMARY

FORM
12-BAR BLUES
(1 CHORUS = 12 BARS)

ARRANGEMENT
PICKUP: 2 BEATS DRUMS
2 CHORUS MELODY
2 CHORUS SOLO
1 CHORUS MELODY
END: 4 M.

HARMONY
D7   G7   A7

SCALE
D BLUES

PLAY "DO IT NOW" WITH YOUR OWN BAND!

"I Just Wanna Be With You" is a *blues swing*. *Swing* is a dance-oriented, big-band style from the 1930s. To hear more swing, listen to artists such as Count Basie, Benny Goodman, the Squirrel Nut Zippers, Diana Krall, Branford Marsalis, Kevin Eubanks, Joanne Brackeen, Cherry Poppin' Daddies, and Big Bad Voodoo Daddy.

LESSON 9
TECHNIQUE/THEORY

Listen to "I Just Wanna Be With You," and then play it along with the recording. This tune is a minor blues, similar to "Do It Now." The saxophones are doubled by the guitar, and the tenor sax adds some harmony. Look for similarities between the three phrases.

PICKUPS

Each phrase of "I Just Wanna Be With You" begins on a weak beat (an eighth note before beat 4), leading to a strong beat (beat 1). Notes leading to a strong beat are called *pickups*. While you are preparing to play, count beats along with the rhythm section. This will help you come in at the right time.

Feel the pulse and count out loud. You come in after the third beat.

Breathe in during the tune's count-off. Draw enough breath so that you can play the first phrase with a good sound.

ARTICULATION: ACCENTS

Notes marked with accent (>) articulations are played louder than the rest so that they stand out. They are often the highest notes in the phrase.

Accents can make a phrase sound more spirited and energize a performance. Use them sparingly. If every note is accented, then nothing will stand out.

To accent a note, blow a sudden puff of air, as if you were fogging a window with warm air. Use a "tah" attack, like legato, but with a stronger T. Accented notes are held for their full value.

Practice accents along with the recording. Make accented notes stand out from the unaccented notes.

Accenting some of the notes in "I Just Wanna Be With You" will make the melody come alive—especially accenting notes that are unexpected, on beats that would ordinarily be weak, such as any eighth note off a beat, or beat 4. Practice it along with the recording. Make your accented notes stand out from the others.

LISTEN **14** PLAY

PRACTICE TIP
Practice slowly. Before you can play something fast, you must be able to play it slowly. Practice your fingerings, and try to hear the notes in your head before you play them.

LESSON 10
LEARNING THE GROOVE

LISTEN **13** PLAY

Listen to "I Just Wanna Be With You" and focus on the cymbals. This tune is a shuffle, like "Do It Now."
There is a triplet feel under each beat. The main difference is that in this tune, the middle note in the triplet
is left out. This is common in swing.

Shuffle
("Do It Now")

Swing Shuffle
("I Just Wanna...")

This syncopated "push-pull" feel is basic to jazz and r&b. Sometimes this feel is called a "double shuffle"
because the drummer plays the same rhythm with both hands. In swing, the bass player usually plays a
"walking" quarter-note bass line.

PRACTICE TIP

Record your practice. Use a small cassette or MiniDisc recorder, and record yourself playing
along with the CD. Then listen to your recording. How accurately and consistently are you
playing?

HOOKING UP TO SWING

Listen to "I Just Wanna Be With You." Find the beat, tap your foot, and click your right-hand keys along with
the backbeat:

LISTEN **13** PLAY

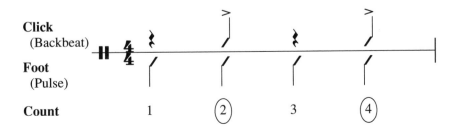

This tune has a swing feel, so count triplets on each beat as you play along with the backbeat. When you are ready, do this along with the recording. The circles show where to click. The hi-hat matches your counting.

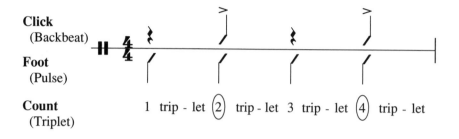

Click swing eighth notes (see lesson 6).

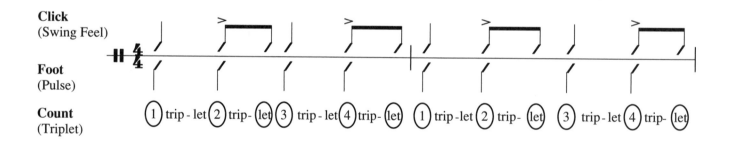

LEARNING "I JUST WANNA BE WITH YOU"

In this tune, the final note of the first measure is accented. Notes on the ordinarily weak beat 4 are usually not stressed, so this comes as a surprise—an interruption of the expected pulse. A rhythm such as this is called a *syncopation*. Syncopation is an important part of swing.

Click the actual rhythms of the melody. When you are ready, click along with the recording. Accent the notes that are marked.

Click
(Melody Rhythms)

Foot
(Pulse)

Count
(Triplets)

Play the actual part along with the recording. Tap your foot and count in your head, as you play. Use accents, and hook up with the groove.

LESSON 11
IMPROVISATION

FORM AND ARRANGEMENT

Listen to "I Just Wanna Be With You," and follow the form. This tune is another 12-bar blues. The form of each chorus is twelve measures long and divided into three phrases, just like "Do It Now."

Listen to "I Just Wanna Be With You." Is there an introduction or ending? What part of the form did these added sections come from? Here is the arrangement used on the recording:

The intro and ending come from the form's last four measures. On the recording, the band chose to play the ending twice. This kind of repeated ending is called a *tag ending*.

Sometimes, a band may decide to "tag a tune" (play a tag ending) several times, building energy with each repetition. If things are going well and everyone is in the mood, a band may even make an ending longer than the rest of the tune. This is a place where people really let loose and have fun playing. When you listen to music, pay attention to what a band is doing at the end of a tune.

SCALES: B BLUES

The B blues scale is a good one for this tune. Play it on your saxophone.

Practice the notes of the B blues scale over a wider range. Notice that it starts on a D. If you can, extend this range even farther, lower and higher.

B Blues Practice

LISTEN **14** PLAY

Practice the B blues scale through this big melodic range, up and down, with the recording. Play each note in steady time, one per beat, and play as evenly as you can. Some notes, especially blue notes such as the F-natural, will jump out at you. Use these notes when you create your own solo.

CALL AND RESPONSE

1. Echo each phrase, exactly as you hear it.
2. Improvise an answer to each phrase. Imitate the sound and rhythmic feel of the phrase you hear, and use the notes from the B blues scale.

Write out a few of your own ideas. Use the B blues scale.

LISTEN **14** PLAY

Create a 2-chorus solo using any techniques you have learned. Memorize your solo, and practice it along with the recording.

SAXOPHONE PART

Play "I Just Wanna Be With You" while reading from the written saxophone part. Play it as written. The guitar doubles the saxes at the melody and plays chords during the improvisation choruses.

LEAD SHEET

Play "I Just Wanna Be With You" from the lead sheet

INTRO/ENDING   Though this lead sheet doesn't show an introduction or ending, you and your band can create your own. The intro can be just drums, as you saw in "Do It Now," or it can come from the last line of the tune, as it does in the recording of this tune. Tag the ending at least three times, repeating the last four measures of the written part.

Since the melody is relatively short in length (twelve measures), you might want to play it twice when you are playing this tune with your own band. Play the pickups whenever you play the melody. You may or may not want to include them in your solo.

CHAPTER III
DAILY PRACTICE ROUTINE

ARTICULATIONS: STACCATO (SWING STYLE)

In swing, staccato is marked with a (ʌ). To play staccato notes in swing, your tongue should move as if you were saying "tut."

Practice swing staccato articulation along with the recording. In this exercise, the staccato markings help emphasize the backbeat.

The recorded version of "I Just Wanna Be With You" uses a combination of staccato and accented notes. Articulating these notes differently energizes the whole melody line. Try to make each articulation stand out. Practice the articulations as shown, and then play it along with the recording.

Saxophone Sound

Using different "syllables," such as "tah," "tut," and "hut," will help you make your notes sound unique. There are also many other factors at work here that will affect the sound of your horn.

Here are some of the factors.
1. your diaphragm (the "support system")
2. how the air starts in your lungs
3. the shape your throat and mouth make as the air passes through them
4. how much mouthpiece is inside your mouth
5. the shape of your bottom lip against the reed
6. how much downward pressure your top teeth exert
7. how much upward pressure your bottom teeth exert

To get a good sound, imagine that you are blowing warm air through your saxophone, as if you were saying "haaaaaah." You can only do this if everything is relaxed, and your throat is open and relaxed. If anything is restricted, as if you were saying "heeuuh," less air will move, your breath will be colder, and your sound won't be as good.

Practice long tones on your saxophone every day, and try to get as full and as warm a sound as you can. Here is an example of the kind of exercise you should do regularly. This one combines practicing long tones with practicing the B blues scale. Keep repeating this exercise for the whole track. Baritone sax players may prefer to play this down an octave.

CHORDS

The lead sheet to "I Just Wanna Be With You" includes four different chords. The first three are *minor seventh chords* and the last one (F♯7) is a dominant seventh chord. The improvised solo makes good use of chord tones.

Practice chord tones with the recording. Notice how different the dominant seventh chord (F♯7 in the last measure) sounds—especially its note A-sharp. The different chord sound and the change in the groove make the last measure stand out and give the tune a unique character. It also helps the last measure to lead back to the first measure for when the form repeats. This is called a *turnaround* because it "turns the form around" back to the beginning.

IMPROVISING USING CHORD TONES

Practice this sax solo and then play it along with the recording. Notice the use of chord tones.

Create some of your own chord-tone licks.

Create a 2-chorus solo using any techniques you have learned. Memorize your solo and practice it along with the recording.

SOLO PRACTICE

Practice the recorded saxophone solo to "I Just Wanna Be With You." When you are ready, play along with the recording.

MEMORIZE

Work on playing your own, personal interpretation of the melody of "I Just Wanna Be With You," with your own articulations and phrasing. Record yourself playing it along with the CD. Next, work on playing your own solos based on its chord progression, song form, and groove. Record your solos. Write down your favorite one and memorize it.

SUMMARY

FORM	ARRANGEMENT	HARMONY	SCALE
12-Bar Blues (1 chorus = 12 bars)	Intro: 4 m. 2 Chorus Melody 2 Chorus Solo 1 Chorus Melody End: 8 m.	B–7 E–7 F#–7 F#7	B Blues

PLAY "I JUST WANNA BE WITH YOU" WITH YOUR OWN BAND!

"Leave Me Alone" is a *funk* tune. Funk has its roots in New Orleans street music. It started in the 1960s and is a combination of rock, r&b, Motown, jazz, and blues. Funk has also influenced many rap artists. To hear more funk, listen to artists such as James Brown, Tower of Power, Kool and the Gang, the Yellowjackets, Chaka Khan, Tina Turner, and the Red Hot Chili Peppers.

LESSON 13
TECHNIQUE/THEORY

Listen to "Leave Me Alone" and play along with the recording. Try to match the saxophone playing the melody.

ARTICULATION: LEGATO

Notes marked with legato (–) articulations in jazz and pop styles are played for their full rhythmic value. Legato marks are similar to slurs, but the articulations are marked on individual notes, rather than whole phrases. When you are *sustaining* (holding) a legato note, counting eighth notes as you play will help you to be sure it lasts for its full duration—all the way up to the rest.

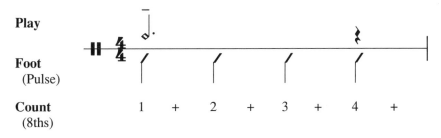

Practice playing notes legato along with the recording. Start and stop your notes as precisely as you can.

Long, legato notes in a melody let listeners hear the rhythm section playing the groove. Short, staccato notes help the melody sound more part of the rhythm section. You can use a combination of both kinds of articulation.

Practice this articulation exercise with the recording.

LONG PHRASES AND BREATHING

Try to play each 4-measure phrase of "Leave Me Alone" in a single breath. This will give each phrase a feeling of continuity. You will need to take a deep breath before you begin each phrase.

When you are looking at a new piece of music and trying to determine where to breathe, the first place to try is during rests. If you need to breathe before you see a rest, look for any natural place in the phrase, in which the phrase or the sense of forward motion won't sound interrupted. You can mark these places with optional breath marks (ʼ). Only breathe there if you have to.

Practice the melody to "Leave Me Alone" with the recording, and try to breathe only at the end of each 4-bar phrase. If you need to breathe earlier, do so only at the optional breath marks.

LESSON 14
LEARNING THE GROOVE

HOOKING UP TO FUNK

LISTEN **17** P L A Y

Listen to "Leave Me Alone." This funk groove has its roots in New Orleans street music—funky march music played on marching instruments (snare drums, bass drums, and so on) still found in the Mardi Gras parades each spring. Many New Orleans artists were important to the development of funk.

Funk rhythms are played with less of a swing feel than blues. There is an underlying sixteenth-note feel, similar to rock, so count "1 e + a, 2 e + a, 3 e + a, 4 e + a," as you play. In funk, the backbeat (beats 2 and 4) is especially accented, usually by the snare drum.

This exercise will help you hook up to funk. Play along with the recording and match the saxophone. The music is written out below. Find the beat, and play the melody. It emphasizes the strong, funk backbeat.

LISTEN **19** P L A Y

SYNCOPATIONS AND ARTICULATIONS

How you articulate syncopations changes how they feel in the groove. In this next example, each lick is played legato and then staccato. Give each one a unique sound. Echo each lick exactly as you hear it, focusing on articulations. You may find that they are easier to hear than to read, so listen carefully and try to copy what you hear.

LESSON 15
IMPROVISATION

FORM AND ARRANGEMENT

Listen to "Leave Me Alone," and follow the form. This funk tune follows the 12-bar blues form.

 LISTEN **17** PLAY

On the recording, the arrangement begins with a 4-measure introduction, featuring the rhythm section playing the groove.

SCALES: E BLUES

The E blues scale is a good choice for use with this tune. Play it on your saxophone.

Practice the notes of the E blues scale over a wider range.

CHORDS

The chords to "Leave Me Alone" are all the same type: dominant seven chords, which you saw in chapter 2. These chords have the same sound, with the same *intervals*—the distances between pitches. The only change is that they are *transposed*; they begin on different notes. When you improvise, favor the chord tones of the symbol shown above the staff. This is called "making the changes," or interpreting the song's chords in your own way.

Practice the chord tones to "Leave Me Alone." Below each tone is an interval number showing the note's relationship to the chord root. Since all chords in this tune are dominant-7 chords, the interval numbers are the same: root, 3, 5, flat-7.

| Root | 3 | 5 | ♭7 | Root | 3 | 5 | ♭7 | Root | 3 | 5 | ♭7 |

RIFFS

Another good improvisation technique is to create a lick and then repeat it over and over. This repetition of a lick is called a *riff*. The lick's notes may come from a scale, from chord tones, from melody notes, or a combination of all three.

In the next exercise, we will play a riff built on this lick. Practice it until you can play it easily.

Echo each riff exactly as you hear it.

LISTEN 21 PLAY

Listen   Play

PERFORMANCE TIP

In blues, riffs work really well during a solo. They create musical tension, and the audience starts wondering how many times it will repeat before something new happens. The listeners move forward to the edge of their seats, just waiting for a temporary conclusion—something that will relieve the musical tension and expectation that has been created.

WRITE YOUR OWN SINGLE RIFF SOLO

Create your own riff-based solo to "Leave Me Alone." Make sure the riff you create sounds good over all the chords. Write it out, and practice it along with the recording.

LISTEN 18 PLAY

TRANSPOSING LICKS

To make a single lick sound good over several different chords, you have to keep it simple and only use a couple of pitches. If you want to use a more complex riff, you can transpose the lick to different notes, similar to how the dominant-7 chords earlier were transposed to begin on different roots.

Practice this lick a few times until you can play it easily. Since it is based on the tune's first chord (**E7**), you can think of it as being in the "original" key. Interval numbers are shown below each note.

To transpose this lick, move its root to the root of each new chord (**A7** and **B7**), and then use the same intervals to find the other notes. Practice the lick based on all three chords until you can play them easily.

Echo each riff exactly as you hear it.

WRITE YOUR OWN TRANSPOSING RIFF SOLO

Create your own riff-based solo to "Leave Me Alone." Transpose the same riff over all the chords. Write it out, and practice it along with the recording.

LESSON 16
READING

SAXOPHONE PART

Play "Leave Me Alone" along with the recording, using the written saxophone part.

CUE NOTES The small notes in measures 1 to 4 are *cue notes* showing the bass part (written out in treble clef). Read along with the bass, and use the cue notes to help you come in on time. If you play baritone, you may want to play this bass line instead of the melody.

LEAVE ME ALONE
Eb SAXOPHONE PART
By MATT MARVUGLIO

LEAD SHEET

Play "Leave Me Alone" and follow along with the lead sheet. Create your own riff-based solo. Try transposing the licks by ear.

PRACTICE TIP

Memorizing your notes makes it easier to follow arrangement directions, such as "D.S. al ⊕."

CHAPTER IV
DAILY PRACTICE ROUTINE

BENDING PITCHES

Raising or lowering the pitch of a note is often referred to as *bending* a note. Most saxophonists can bend most notes down a lot, and up at least a little. Relaxing or "loosening" the pressure of the embouchure lowers the pitch. Increasing the pressure of the embouchure raises the pitch.

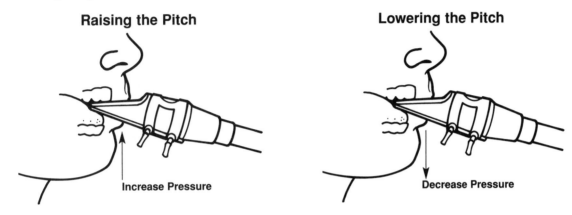

Raising the Pitch   **Lowering the Pitch**

Increase Pressure   **Decrease Pressure**

Play a middle C-sharp on your saxophone for four beats at a medium-slow tempo. Play it straight, without bending the pitch.

Play the same note again. Begin the note normally, then try bending the pitch downwards.

Play the same note again, and after beginning the note normally, try bending the pitch upwards.

PERFORMANCE TIP

As you bend the pitch of a note downwards, you'll have to blow more air through your saxophone just to sustain the note. You should be prepared to supply enough air to keep the note sounding!

Bends are good effects when you are improvising. They will also help you play in tune. If you are having trouble bending your notes downwards, your normal embouchure may be too loose.

BEND PRACTICE

Play along with the saxophone in the recording. Try to match its intonation exactly, starting and ending each note on pitch.

INTONATION/INTERVAL PRACTICE

This exercise will also help your intonation. Play this next exercise twice. First, play the top staff, then play the bottom staff. If you hear any "pulses" or "beats" between your note and the recording, it means that you are not playing in tune. Keep in tune with the track.

FUNK RHYTHMS

LISTEN **18** PLAY

Practice this solo with the recording. Choose a combination of articulations to make your part groove with the rhythm section. Write your articulations into the score below.

MAKING THE CHANGES

This solo draws its notes from three different sources. During **E7** measures, the notes come from the E blues scale. During the **A7** measures, the notes come from the chord tones of **A7**. During the **B7** measure, the notes come from chord tones of **B7**. Practice it alone first, and when you're ready, play it with the recording.

LISTEN **18** PLAY

SOLO PRACTICE

Practice the recorded saxophone solo to "Leave Me Alone." Before you play, read along with the recording, and finger the notes on saxophone without blowing—just clicking the keys. When you are ready, play along with the recording. If you can't hit the high G, bring it down an octave.

LISTEN **17** P L A Y

MEMORIZE

LISTEN **18** PLAY

Create your own solo using any of the techniques you have learned, and write it out. Practice it, memorize it, and then record yourself playing the whole tune along with the recording.

SUMMARY

FORM
12-BAR BLUES
(1 CHORUS = 12 BARS)

ARRANGEMENT
INTRO: 4 M.
2 CHORUS MELODY
2 CHORUS SOLO
1 CHORUS MELODY

HARMONY

E7 A7 B7

SCALE

E BLUES

PLAY "LEAVE ME ALONE" WITH YOUR OWN BAND!

"Affordable" is another funk tune, but it is lighter, with more of a feeling of open space. This style is popular with smooth-jazz artists. To hear more light funk, listen to artists such as David Sanborn, Earl Klugh, Walter Beasley, the Rippingtons, Dave Grusin, Kenny G, Bob James, and Anita Baker.

LESSON 17
TECHNIQUE/THEORY

LISTEN **24** PLAY

Listen to "Affordable," and then play along with the recording. Try to match the saxophone on the melody.

DYNAMICS

The melody of "Affordable" is made mostly of long, drawn out notes. The sax player on the recording makes this melody more interesting by changing the notes' *dynamics*—their loudness and softness. In this tune, the last notes of each phrase generally *decrescendo* (gradually become softer). The notation for decrescendos is a wedge (sometimes called a *hairpin*) opening to the left (>). This shows where the sound should be louder (above the lines' widest point) and where it should be softer (above where the lines meet). The opposite of a decrescendo is a *crescendo* (gradually growing louder), which opens to the right (<).

Practice the melody to "Affordable" with the recording, and decrescendo at the end of phrases 1, 2, and 4. Notice how dynamics help to shape the melody.

LISTEN **24** PLAY

LESSON 18
LEARNING THE GROOVE

HOOKING UP TO LIGHT FUNK

LISTEN **24** PLAY

Listen to "Affordable." This groove is built around eighth notes, with some syncopated sixteenths in the B section. Notice that the band hooks up with the bass drum.

To learn this feel, practice counting sixteenths, leaving out the middle two sixteenths of each beat. Count out loud, along with a metronome or click track on the quarter-note pulse.

1   e   +   a   2   (e) (+)   a   3 think think a   4   a   1   a   2   a   3   a   4   a

"Affordable" is a *light* funk tune. Like all funk music, eighth notes are played straight, not with a swing feel. The rhythm section plays fewer notes than they do in other styles of music. This makes the saxophone stand out even more than it does on the other tunes. What other elements of funk do you notice?

Listen to "Affordable." Find the pulse, and feel the sixteenth-note subdivisions. Notice that the backbeat is still emphasized, but it is lighter than it was in heavy funk.

SAXOPHONE IN THE RHYTHM SECTION

To hook up to a groove, try playing the rhythm section's parts along with the recording. This sax line combines the bass, guitar, and keyboard parts. Feel the backbeat and the sixteenth notes as you play.

There are two different grooves in this tune. Play this first riff during phrases 1, 2, and 4, and at the introduction.

Play this riff during phrase 3.

LESSON 19
IMPROVISATION

FORM AND ARRANGEMENT

Listen to "Affordable," and follow the 16-bar form.

LISTEN **24** PLAY

From practicing the keyboard, guitar, and bass parts, you can tell that there are two primary musical ideas in this tune. When you play the melody you can hear that there are two contrasting sections. Idea A is very sparse. It lasts for eight measures, with two phrases of sax melody. Idea B is in a more regular rhythm. It lasts for four measures. Then idea A returns for four measures. This form can be described as "AABA."

Listen to the whole tune. Sing the melody while the saxophone plays the solo, and keep your place in the form. What is the arrangement on the recording? Is there an introduction or ending? Check your answer against the summary at the end of this chapter.

SCALES: E MAJOR AND MINOR PENTATONIC

The E major pentatonic scale will work well for improvising on this tune's A sections.

The E minor pentatonic scale will work well for improvising on this tune's B section.

CALL AND RESPONSE

1. Echo each phrase, exactly as you hear it.
2. Improvise an answer to each phrase. Imitate the sound and rhythmic feel of the phase you hear, and use the notes from the E pentatonic scales.

EMBELLISHING THE MELODY

The song melody is an excellent source of ideas for notes and licks. Whenever you play the melody, you contribute to the musical mood. The melody identifies the spirit and character of the song.

Think of the song melody as a compass. As you improvise, use it as your guide. Keep the melody at your solo's center, and improvise by adding or removing a few notes, or by varying their rhythm. Such changes are called *embellishments*.

Practice this embellished version of "Affordable." When you're ready, practice it along with the recording.

Try playing the embellished version above "against" the original song melody. You can feel the added notes when you play them along with the original melody track.

Write out your own embellished version of the melody. Use the E pentatonic scales and the melody itself as sources for notes.

Create a 1-chorus solo using any techniques you have learned. Memorize your solo, and practice it along with the recording.

LESSON 20
READING

SAXOPHONE PART

♭ SAXOPHONE PART

Part label. The written parts you have been using were written specifically for E-flat saxophones. The notes have been *transposed* to suit the saxophone's tuning. The saxophone is a *transposing instrument* in E-flat, which means that the notes are written transposed a minor third below where they sound on *non-transposing* (or *concert*) instruments, such as the guitar, bass, or keyboard. This is done because the strongest registers of the E-flat saxophones are a bit higher than will fit on a regular staff. If the notes were written where they sound, sax players would have to read a lot more ledger lines. Transposing the part reduces the number of ledger lines and makes reading easier.

Since the alto and baritone saxophones are transposed to E-Flat, when they read a written C, it sounds a concert E-flat. This means that the melody notes in the written saxophone part will be different than the written melody in the guitar part, which is non-transposing. Make sure your part is labeled E-Flat Saxophone Part, or variations such as: E♭, E♭ Part, Alto, Alto Sax, Bari Sax, Baritone Saxophone, or others.

The part that follows includes cue notes showing the bass and keyboard parts. They have been transposed to E-flat. This means that a sax player can read the cue notes, but a bass or keyboard player would have to transpose them back up a third, if they are to sound correctly. If their key signature was different, it would mean that it was being presented in concert pitch.

Play "Affordable" while reading the saxophone part, and solo where indicated. Use the cue notes to help you keep your place. Baritone players may want to try the bass line instead of the melody.

Affordable

E♭ Saxophone Part

By Matt Marvuglio

LEAD SHEET

Play "Affordable" while reading the lead sheet.

LISTEN **28** PLAY

AFFORDABLE

Eb SAX

BY MATT MARVUGLIO

CHAPTER V
DAILY PRACTICE ROUTINE

VIBRATO

Another way to add interest to a melody (especially on notes of long duration) is to use *vibrato*. Vibrato is a slight, controlled vibration of a note's pitch, giving it a singing quality. In the older styles, such as early jazz, vibrato was typically wide and rapid. In more contemporary saxophone playing styles, vibrato is generally used more sparingly.

In contemporary pop, r&b, rock, and jazz saxophone playing styles, the speed and depth (variation of pitch) of vibrato are more varied. Many times, long notes begin straight, and then vibrato is added gradually. By listening to a lot of music, you will develop your own sense for when to use vibrato.

To add vibrato to a note, increase and decrease your embouchure pressure, raising and lowering the pitch.

Practice long tones along with the recording. Start each note straight, then gradually add more and more vibrato to it, following the curvy line.

DYNAMICS AND VIBRATO

Try combining vibrato with dynamics, adding just a touch of vibrato at the end of phrases 1, 2, and 4. Don't overdo it! Just a little vibrato will sound great.

PENTATONIC SCALE PRACTICE

LISTEN **28** PLAY

Create a solo using the tune's chords and notes of the E pentatonic scales, shown below the saxophone staff. Try using different rhythms that hook up to the light funk groove. Practice your solo with the recording.

E7

MEMORIZE

LISTEN **28** PLAY

Create your own solo using any of the techniques you have learned, and write it out. Practice it, memorize it, and then record yourself playing the whole tune along with the CD.

SUMMARY

FORM
16-BAR ABBA
(1 CHORUS = 16 BARS)
A: 4 M.
B: 4 M.

ARRANGEMENT
INTRO: 8 M.
1 CHORUS MELODY
1 CHORUS SOLO
1 CHORUS MELODY

HARMONY

SCALE

PLAY "AFFORDABLE" WITH YOUR OWN BAND!

"Don't Look Down" is a *hard rock* tune. Hard rock first appeared in the late 1960s. It has characteristic heavy bass, long, drawn-out chords, and amplified instruments. To hear more hard rock, listen to artists such as Aerosmith, Metallica, Powerman 5000, the Allman Brothers Band, Rob Zombie, Godsmack, 311, Stone Temple Pilots, Black Crowes, Steve Vai, and Smashing Pumpkins.

LESSON 21
TECHNIQUE/THEORY

LISTEN **29** PLAY

Listen to "Don't Look Down," and then play the melody along with the recording. The saxes are doubled by the guitar. This tune has two different parts.

The first part has these four phrases.

The second part has a riff that repeats four times.

It ends with the bass riff, played twice.

HIGH REGISTER

The high register can lend a great deal of energy and intensity to music, especially when it is played loudly. For hard rock, you may want to transpose part or all of the melody up an octave, and use some high notes in your solo.

Practice "Don't Look Down" with some of the phrases transposed to the higher octave, and notice their increased intensity. Focus on playing in tune.

LESSON 22
LEARNING THE GROOVE

HOOKING UP TO HARD ROCK

Listen to "Don't Look Down." This tune has a standard rock/metal groove. It is a heavy feel, with very simple drum and bass parts. These parts must be simple because they are intended to be played in large arenas, where echoes would make busier parts sound muddy. It's a case of "less is more."

During the solos, the guitar doubles the bass, playing power chords in the second part. The keyboard plays sustained chords with an organ sound.

LISTEN 30 PLAY

Listen to the first part of "Don't Look Down." Click the right-hand keys along with the quarter-note pulse and the left-hand keys along with the backbeat.

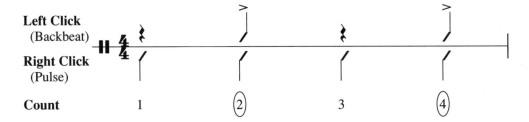

Try the same thing again. This time count the sixteenth notes out loud: 1e+a, 2e+a, 3e+a, 4e+a.

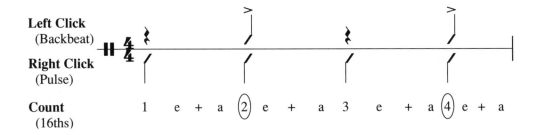

LEARNING "DON'T LOOK DOWN"

In the first part of this tune, the bass guitar plays a syncopated sixteenth-note riff. You hook up with that riff while you play the melody, and then you actually play the riff at the ending.

First, practice clicking the rhythms.

Next, play the actual notes. Hook up with the rhythm section. If you like, you can play this riff instead of the melody along with the A section of the full-band track.

The second part of this tune also has a syncopated sixteenth-note figure. Practice clicking the rhythms to this lick (also used at the Intro).

Practice the notes.

Practice the whole tune along with the recording, and hook up with the rhythm section.

LESSON 23
IMPROVISATION

FORM AND ARRANGEMENT

LISTEN **29** PLAY

Listen to the recording, and try to figure out the form and arrangement by ear. How long does each section of the form last? Is there an introduction or ending? For how many measures or beats does each chord last? Write down as much information as you can. Check your answers against the summary at the end of this chapter.

This tune has a 20-bar AB form. Part A has an active riff that builds a lot of tension. It lasts for sixteen measures. Part B is less active than the first part. It lasts for four measures. There is a 4-measure introduction at the beginning of the tune. It comes from the B section.

SCALES: E MAJOR AND MINOR PENTATONIC

The E major pentatonic scale will work well for improvising on this tune's A section.

The E minor pentatonic scale will work well for improvising on this tune's B section.

Practice both these scales. You can use both of them when you improvise, depending upon the chord.

CALL AND RESPONSE

Mixing Chord Tones and Pentatonic Scales

1. Echo the rhythm of each phrase exactly.
2. Improvise an answer to each phrase. Copy the rhythms of the recorded licks but choose your own notes, based on the source indicated above the staff.

Write out a few of your own ideas.

Create a 1-chorus solo using any techniques you have learned. Memorize your solo, and practice it with the recording.

SAXOPHONE PART

Play "Don't Look Down" along with the recording. Use the written saxophone part.

First and second ending markings. The first time you play these measures, play the *first ending*—the measures under the number 1. Then return to the begin-repeat sign (‖:). The second time you play these measures, skip the first ending and play the *second ending*—the measures under the number 2. Then, continue through the rest of the form.

LISTEN **33** PLAY

DON'T LOOK DOWN

E♭ Saxophone Part

BY MATT MARVUGLIO

PERFORMANCE TIP

When you practice from a lead sheet, use it to help you keep your place. Even when you solo, follow the music as you play. This will help you to keep track of the form, so you can memorize it.

LEAD SHEET

Play your own part to "Don't Look Down," and follow along with the lead sheet.

CHAPTER VI
DAILY PRACTICE ROUTINE

EMBELLISHMENT PRACTICE

Practice embellishing the melody to "Don't Look Down." Play the written 4-bar embellished melody and then your own 4-bar embellished melody. Include the original melody notes, on their original beats, in your embellished melody.

SOLO PRACTICE

Practice the recorded solo along with the CD.

MEMORIZE

LISTEN **33** PLAY

Create your own solo using any of the techniques you have learned, and write it out. Practice it, memorize it, and then record yourself playing the whole tune along with the recording.

Summary

Form	Arrangement	Harmony	Scale
20-Bar AB form (1 chorus = 20 bars) A: 16 m. B: 4 m.	Intro: 4 m. 1 Chorus Melody 1 Chorus Solo 1 Chorus Melody End: 2 m.	D A E	E Major Pentatonic E Minor Pentatonic

Play "Don't Look Down" with your own band!

"Take Your Time" is a *bossa nova* tune. Bossa nova began in Brazil, combining American jazz and an Afro-Brazilian form of dance music called *samba*. To hear more bossa nova, listen to Stan Getz, Antonio Carlos Jobim, Eliane Elias, Astrud Gilberto, Flora Purim, Dave Valentine, and Spyro Gyra.

LESSON 25
TECHNIQUE/THEORY

Listen to "Take Your Time" on the recording. The melody is in two long phrases. Practice it along with the recording, and try to match the saxophones.

PRACTICE TIP

Take a deep breath before you play each of the above phrases. If you begin each phrase with enough air, you'll be able to play those low notes with a clear, full tone.

LOW REGISTER

Practicing low notes will help you develop a full sound in the middle and high registers as well. These notes require more air to be blown through the horn. Since most of the keys are closed, the air must resonate through the entire length of the instrument in order to sound, which gives the lower notes their fuller, more resonant quality.

Practice this low-register exercise along with the recording. Maintain a big, full sound.

LISTEN **35** P L A Y

LESSON 26
LEARNING THE GROOVE

HOOKING UP TO BOSSA NOVA

Listen to "Take Your Time." This tune is a bossa nova, a style of music that originated in Brazil. Throughout the tune, a 2-bar rhythmic pattern repeats. This repeating pattern is an essential part of bossa nova. The drum plays it on a rim click.

LISTEN **34** PLAY

Repeating rhythmic structures are at the heart of much African-based music, including Afro-Caribbean and most South and Latin American styles.

> ### PRACTICE TIP
>
> A good way to practice hooking up with a tune is to play all the other instruments' parts.

Listen to the drums on the recording and follow the drumbeat below. Drummers will occasionally vary the pattern slightly as they play through a song, but this is the basic beat to "Take Your Time." Notice that the snare drum (rim click) plays the repeating rhythmic pattern above.

LISTEN **34** PLAY

Hi-Hat
Snare Drum
(Rim Click)
Bass Drum

Practice the bass drum part along with the recording. Match the bass drum rhythms exactly.

The bass guitar rhythm is similar to the bass drum rhythm. It is a 2-bar rhythmic pattern that continues throughout the tune. Practice the bass guitar part along with the recording.

Play the snare drum rhythms, which sound the bossa nova pattern you saw at the beginning of this lesson. Hook up with the bossa nova groove.

Play the keyboard's own 2-bar rhythm. You will be playing the top note of each keyboard chord. Match the keyboard on the recording.

CHALLENGE

Try to figure out the guitar's part by ear.

LESSON 27
IMPROVISATION

FORM AND ARRANGEMENT

LISTEN **34** PLAY

Listen to "Take Your Time," and try to figure out the form and arrangement by ear. Then continue with this chapter.

This tune follows a 16-bar AB form. Each phrase of the melody lasts for eight measures.

What is the arrangement on the recording? Figure it out by ear, and then check your answer against the summary at the end of this chapter.

SCALES: B PENTATONIC

For the first twelve measures of this tune (over the **B–7** and **CMAJ7** chords), we will use the *B minor pentatonic* scale to improvise. Practice this scale on your saxophone.

Practice the B minor pentatonic scale throughout your entire range.

In the last four measures (over the **BMAJ7** chord), solo using notes from the *B major pentatonic* scale. Major pentatonic scales work well when improvising on major or major-7 chords. Practice this scale on your saxophone.

Practice the B major pentatonic scale throughout your entire range.

CALL AND RESPONSE

1. Echo each phrase, exactly as you hear it.
2. Improvise an answer to each phrase. Imitate the sound and rhythmic feel of the phrase you hear, and use the notes from the B pentatonic scales.

LISTEN **36** PLAY

Write out some of your own ideas. Use notes from the B pentatonic scales.

LISTEN 35 PLAY

Create a 1-chorus solo using any techniques you have learned. Memorize your solo, practice it along with the recording, and then record it.

LESSON 28
READING

SAXOPHONE PART

$\frac{2}{/\!/}$ Two-measure repeat. Repeat the previously notated two measures.

Play "Take Your Time," and use the written part. Alternately, baritone sax could play the bass line and alto sax could play the keyboard line. Use the full band track (track 34), if you do.

LISTEN 35 PLAY

TAKE YOUR TIME
Eb Saxophone Part

By Matt Marvuglio

LEAD SHEET

Play "Take Your Time," and follow the lead sheet.

CHAPTER VII
DAILY PRACTICE ROUTINE

CHORD TONES AND TENSIONS

A *tension* note is an extension of a chord. The example below shows extended chord arpeggios. They are another good source of notes to use in your solos.

1. Echo each phrase, exactly as you hear it. Notice the use of tensions.
2. Improvise an answer to each phrase. Imitate the sound and rhythmic feel of the phrase you hear, and use chord tones. Try using the same tension notes as you hear on the recording.

Write out some of your own ideas. Use notes from the B pentatonic scales and from the chord tones and tensions of B–7, BMAJ7, and CMAJ7.

SAXOPHONE SOLO

Practice the recorded solo along with the CD. Notice the use of long tones, chord tones, and tensions.

MEMORIZE

LISTEN **35** PLAY

Create your own solo using any of the techniques you have learned, and write it out. Practice it, memorize it, and then record yourself playing the whole tune along with the recording.

Summary

Form	Arrangement	Harmony	Scale
16-Bar AB form (1 Chorus = 16 bars) A: 8 m. B: 8 m.	Intro: 8 m. 2 Chorus Melody 2 Chorus Solo 1 Chorus Melody End: 8 m.	A B B—7 CMAJ7 BMAJ7	B Minor Pentatonic B Major Pentatonic

Play "Take Your Time" with your own band!

"Stop It" is a blues/jazz tune in which *stop time* accents the melody, like a question and answer. Stop time is very common in blues, jazz, and other styles. To hear more stop time blues, listen to artists such as Miles Davis, John Coltrane, Jim Hall, Sarah Vaughn, Bill Evans, Ella Fitzgerald, Louis Armstrong, Abbie Lincoln, Dizzy Gillespie, and Charlie Parker.

LESSON 29
TECHNIQUE/THEORY

Listen to "Stop It," and then play along with the melody. Try to match the saxophones. Notice that there are only three different licks.

ARTICULATION

A way to make this melody come alive is by using different articulations for the licks. The first, third, and fifth lick should all be played legato, with the notes sounding connected to each other. This is often marked with a slur. Only the first note should be articulated.

The second lick (repeated after licks 3 and 5) is made up of five notes with alternating staccato and legato articulations.

The lick at bar 9 is also legato.

Practice the melody along with the recording, articulating these licks as shown above.

LESSON 30
LEARNING THE GROOVE

HOOKING UP TO STOP-TIME BLUES

LISTEN **38** PLAY

Listen to "Stop It." This jazz cymbal beat is at the heart of jazz rhythm. The "spang spang-a-lang" cymbal beat is unique to jazz, and it has been its primary pattern since the 1940s. Its underlying pulse is the same as the shuffle. This pattern has accompanied Louis Armstrong, Count Basie, Miles Davis, John Coltrane, Duke Ellington, and thousands of other jazz artists.

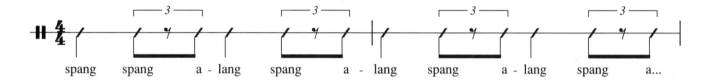

STOP TIME

In stop time, the groove is punctuated by *stop time kicks*. These are rhythmic figures, usually just one or two beats long, that punctuate the melody. That is why it is called "stop time"—the melody "stops" or rests.

Play the melody along with the recording. On this tune, the saxophone plays the melody during the stop time sections. Tap the pulse with your foot, and feel the subdivisions. Hook up with the groove.

LISTEN **39** PLAY

REGULAR TIME

During the solos, the rhythm section *plays time*. The drums play a steady beat, the bass *walks* (plays steady quarter notes), and the keyboard and guitar play chords.

The guitar plays chords in a 2-measure pattern. Play the guitar part (the top notes of its chords) along with the recording. Match the guitar's articulation and time feel.

The keyboard also has a repeating 2-measure pattern. Play the keyboard part (the top notes of its chords) along with the recording. Match the keyboard's articulation and time feel, and notice how it hooks up with the guitar part.

LESSON 31
IMPROVISATION

FORM AND ARRANGEMENT

Listen to "Stop It," and try to figure out the form and arrangement by ear. Check your answer against the summary at the end of this chapter.

Check your answer against the summary at the end of this chapter.

SCALES: F-SHARP BLUES

Use the F-sharp blues scale to improvise on this tune.

Practice the notes of the F-sharp blues scale throughout the entire range of your saxophone.

Practice playing the chord tones used in this tune. Notice the extension of the **C#7(#9)** chord.

The **C#7(#9)** chord has a dissonance between the E-natural and the E-sharp. This color is one of the defining elements of the chord progression, and will lend a distinctive color to your solo.

Here is an example of the kind of licks you can play that make use of that dissonance.

CALL AND RESPONSE

1. Echo each phrase, exactly as you hear it.
2. Improvise an answer to each phrase. Imitate the sound and rhythmic feel of the phrase you hear. Use the F-sharp blues scale, chord tones, and tensions.

Write out some of your own ideas. Use chord tones and notes from the F-sharp pentatonic scales.

Create a 2-chorus solo using any techniques you have learned. Memorize your solo and practice it along with the recording.

LESSON 32
READING

SAXOPHONE PART

Play "Stop It" along with the recording, and read from the written saxophone part.

D.C. AL

"From the beginning, and take the coda." Jump to the very first measure of the tune and play from there. When you reach the first coda symbol, skip ahead to the next coda symbol (at the end). This is similar to the "D.S. al Coda," but instead of going to a sign, go to the first measure of the tune.

LISTEN **43** PLAY

LEAD SHEET

Play "Stop It" from the lead sheet.

LISTEN **43** P L A Y

STOP IT

Eb Sax

By Matt Marvuglio

CHAPTER VIII
DAILY PRACTICE ROUTINE

CHORD TONE PRACTICE

Practice this melody, which uses chord tones and tensions of the chords to "Stop It."

CALL AND RESPONSE

1. Echo each phrase, exactly as you hear it.
2. Improvise an answer to each phrase. Use the rhythms shown and choose notes from the chord tones shown below the staff. Be sure to mix up the chord tones, rather than playing them in the order shown.

LISTEN 44 PLAY

Write out a few of your own ideas. Use chord tones and the F-sharp blues scale.

Create a 2-chorus solo using any techniques you have learned. Memorize your solo, and practice it along with the recording.

SOLO PRACTICE

Practice the recorded saxophone solo along with the CD.

MEMORIZE

LISTEN 43 PLAY

Create your own solo using any of the techniques you have learned, and write it out. Practice it, memorize it, and then record yourself playing the whole tune along with the recording.

SUMMARY

FORM	ARRANGEMENT	HARMONY	SCALE
12-Bar Blues (1 chorus = 12 bars)	2 Chorus Melody 4 Chorus Solo 2 Chorus Melody End: 1 m.	F#−7 B−7 C#7(#9)	F# Blues

PLAY "STOP IT" WITH YOUR OWN BAND!

FINAL REMARKS

Congratulations on completing the *Berklee Practice Method.* You now have a good idea of the role of the saxophonist in a band, and have command of the eight grooves and time feels of these tunes. The articulations and the solos that you have learned are important and useful parts of your musical vocabulary. In addition, you have tools and ideas for creating your own solos. This is a great start!

What to do next? Play along with your favorite recordings. Find records that you hear other musicians talking about. Learn these tunes, grooves, and solos. There is a good reason that musicians talk about certain bands, albums, or saxophonists. Continue your theory, reading and technique work. Investigate chord scales and modes. Learn all your key signatures (major and minor), scales, and chord arpeggios.

Develop your concept of what it means to play a saxophone. Realize how important you are as a saxophonist in a band. You have a big responsibility, playing the melody and improvising. It is a powerful position.

Play every day, by yourself and with others, and get the sound in your body.

Keep the beat!

—Jim and Bill

More Fine Publications from Berklee Press